C000277031

The hip flask

The hip flask

short poems from Ireland

edited by Frank Ormsby

woodcuts by Barbara Childs

THE
BLACKSTAFF
PRESS
—
BELFAST

First published in 2000 by
The Blackstaff Press Limited
Blackstaff House, Wildflower Way, Apollo Road
Belfast BT12 6TA, Northern Ireland
with the assistance of
The Arts Council of Northern Ireland

The acknowledgements on pages 131–7
constitute an extension of this copyright page

Printed in England by Biddles Limited

A CIP catalogue record for this book
is available from the British Library

ISBN 0-85640-681-3

www.blackstaffpress.com

for my daughter
Helen

Helen
b. 12 August 1994

The war will soon be over, or so they say.
Five floors below the Friday rush-hour starts.
You're out and breathing. We smile to hear you cry.
Your long fingers curl around our hearts.

The place knows nothing of you and is home.
Indifferent skies look on while August warms
the middle air. We wrap you in your name.
Peace is the way you settle in our arms.

CONTENTS

PREFACE

IN IRELAND the short poem may be said to have its
origins in the Gaelic tradition, particularly in the
nature lyrics – light, immediate, celebratory – of the
sixth and seventh centuries, impromptu responses or
reflections jotted down by monastic scribes in the
margins of the works they had been delegated to tran-
scribe. These lyrics survive, delicate and robust, not
only in their original form, but in the English transla-
tions of scholars and poets and have taken their place
in the canon of Irish literature in both languages.

By contrast, however, the short poem as practised by
Irish poets in the twentieth century has, with a few
individual exceptions, been somewhat marginalised.
Understandably, perhaps, anthologists tend to pass
over the short poem, however engaging and memo-
rable, as less evidently 'substantial' than the more
extended piece. This anthology is an attempt to
redress the balance, to present some of the delights of
an attractive and under-represented form, giving each
poem selected the space to resonate.

How long is a short poem? Since there is no defini-
tive answer, I established the boundary at ten lines, an
arbitrary limit, of course, but not as random as it may
seem. My own sense of the short poem is of an insight
distilled or crystallised, the essence of a mood or emo-
tion caught with memorable concision, the verbal

equivalent – imagistic, aphoristic, epigrammatic – of the brushstroke which evokes the fuller picture, the splash and its ripples. Many of the short poems I have carried around in my head for years, the poems which may be said to have prompted this anthology, create their expansive effects in fewer than ten lines, in some cases considerably fewer, so that the ten-line limit has seemed from the start a natural boundary.

In the interest of range and variety, no poet is represented by more than five poems and I have included a few poems by non-Irish writers on the grounds that they were written in or about Ireland. I have also extracted from sequences or sets of short poems, but only in cases where the poems extracted seemed to me to have a life independent of their context.

FRANK ORMSBY
BELFAST, 2000

W.B. YEATS
1865–1939

AFTER LONG SILENCE

Speech after long silence; it is right,
All other lovers being estranged or dead,
Unfriendly lamplight hid under its shade,
The curtains drawn upon unfriendly night,
That we descant and yet again descant
Upon the supreme theme of Art and Song:
Bodily decrepitude is wisdom; young
We loved each other and were ignorant.

W.B. YEATS

A DRINKING SONG

Wine comes in at the mouth
And love comes in at the eye;
That's all we shall know for truth
Before we grow old and die.
I lift the glass to my mouth,
I look at you, and I sigh.

MEMORY

One had a lovely face,
And two or three had charm,
But charm and face were in vain
Because the mountain grass
Cannot but keep the form
Where the mountain hare has lain.

THE SPUR

You think it horrible that lust and rage
Should dance attention upon my old age;
They were not such a plague when I was young;
What else have I to spur me into song?

W.B. YEATS

THE GREAT DAY

Hurrah for revolution and more cannon-shot!
A beggar upon horseback lashes a beggar on foot.
Hurrah for revolution and cannon come again!
The beggars have changed places, but the lash goes on.

J.M. SYNGE
1871–1909

DREAD

Beside a chapel I'd a room looked down,
Where all the women from the farms and town,
On holy days, and Sundays used to pass
To marriages, and christenings and to Mass.

Then I sat lonely watching score and score,
Till I turned jealous of the Lord next door . . .
Now by this window, where there's none can see,
The Lord God's jealous of yourself and me.

A QUESTION

I asked if I got sick and died, would you
With my black funeral go walking too,
If you'd stand close to hear them talk or pray
While I'm let down in that steep bank of clay.

And, No, you said, for if you saw a crew
Of living idiots, pressing round that new
Oak coffin – they alive, I dead beneath
That board – you'd rave and rend them with your teeth.

AUSTIN CLARKE
1896–1974

PENAL LAW

Burn Ovid with the rest. Lovers will find
A hedge-school for themselves and learn by heart
All that the clergy banish from the mind,
When hands are joined and head bows in the dark.

MONK GIBBON

1896–1987

I TELL HER SHE IS LOVELY

I tell her she is lovely and she laughs,
Shy laughter altogether lovely too;
Knowing, perhaps that it was true before;
And, when she laughs, that it is still more true.

FRANK O'CONNOR
1903–1966

ADVICE TO LOVERS

The way to get on with a girl
Is to drift like a man in a mist,
Happy enough to be caught,
Happy to be dismissed.

Glad to be out of her way,
Glad to rejoin her in bed,
Equally grieved or gay
To learn that she's living or dead.

AFTER THE IRISH
Anonymous, seventh to twelfth centuries

FRANK O'CONNOR

THE KING OF CONNACHT

'Have you seen Hugh,
The Connacht king in the field?'
'All that we saw
Was his shadow under his shield.'

AFTER THE IRISH

PATRICK KAVANAGH
1904–1967

CONSIDER THE GRASS GROWING

Consider the grass growing
As it grew last year and the year before,
Cool about the ankles like summer rivers
When we walked on a May evening through the
    meadows
To watch the mare that was going to foal.

PATRICK KAVANAGH

SANCTITY

To be a poet and not know the trade,
To be a lover and repel all women;
Twin ironies by which great saints are made,
The agonizing pincer-jaws of Heaven.

SAMUEL BECKETT
1906–1989

I WOULD LIKE MY LOVE TO DIE

I would like my love to die
and the rain to be raining on the graveyard
and on me walking the streets
mourning her who thought she loved me.

LOUIS MacNEICE
1907–1963

NIGHT CLUB

After the legshows and the brandies
And all the pick-me-ups for tired
Men there is a feeling
Something more is required.

The lights go down and eyes
Look up across the room;
Salome comes in, bearing
The head of God knows whom.

LOUIS MacNEICE

CORNER SEAT

Suspended in a moving night
The face in the reflected train
Looks at first sight as self-assured
As your own face – But look again:
Windows between you and the world
Keep out the cold, keep out the fright;
Then why does your reflection seem
So lonely in the moving night?

CODA

Maybe we knew each other better
When the night was young and unrepeated
And the moon stood still over Jericho.

So much for the past; in the present
There are moments caught between heart-beats
When maybe we know each other better.

But what is that clinking in the darkness?
Maybe we shall know each other better
When the tunnels meet beneath the mountain.

JOHN HEWITT
1907–1987

LYRIC

Let but a thrush begin
or colour catch my eye,
maybe a spring-woke whin
under a reeling sky,

and all at once I lose
mortality's despair,
having so much to choose
out of the teeming air.

JOHN HEWITT

CHINESE FLUTEPLAYER

The small bronze figure lips a silent flute,
and stillness spreads about him like a lake;
he stands there out of time, and once you look
you are involved, released from mortal state,
because all sense is channelled into sight.
See how light strikes and strokes his rounded brow
and pauses on his dreaming-lidded eyes –
this shell of metal sings for ever now.

GREY AND WHITE

Grey sea, grey sky
two things are bright;
the gull-white foam,
the gull, foam-white.

W.R. RODGERS

1909–1969

THE LOVERS

After the tiff there was stiff silence, till
One word, flung in centre like single stone,
Starred and cracked the ice of her resentment
To its edge. From that stung core opened and
Poured up one outward and widening wave
Of eager and extravagant anger.

THE FOUNTAINS

Suddenly all the fountains in the park
Opened smoothly their umbrellas of water,
Yet there was none but me to miss or mark
Their peacock show, and so I moved away
Uneasily, like one who at a play
Finds himself all alone, and will not stay.

FERGUS ALLEN
b. 1921

WAY BACK THEN

The floor-show ends, lights dim, I tilt the bottle;
The maestro turns, vibrant in black and white,
Confers the boon of his electric ego
And drives the music forward through the night.

So here I sit, champagne glass in my hand,
Afloat on rhythms of the Latin south,
Drawn by inexorable tidal currents
To the pearl harbour of your smiling mouth.

BRENDAN BEHAN
1923–1964

LONELINESS

The tang of blackberries,
wet with rain
on the hilltop.

In the silence of the prison
the clear whistle of the train.

The happy whisperings of lovers
to the lonely one.

FRANCIS HARVEY
b. 1925

STORM PETREL

has spent a lifetime trying to perfect
the technique of being able to walk

on water. He scans the surface of the sea
myopically and keeps dipping his feet

in the waves to test them for the exact
temperature at which faith once sustained

the weight of Peter's body on the Sea
of Galilee forgetting that faith is not

an acquired technique in his unremitting
efforts to live up to a famous name.

RICHARD MURPHY
b. 1927

LULLABY

Before you'd given death a name
Like bear or crocodile, death came

To take your mother out one night.
But when she'd said her last good night

You cried, 'I don't want you to go,'
So in her arms she took you too.

THOMAS KINSELLA
b. 1928

FIRE AND ICE

Two creatures face each other, fixed in song,
Satyr and nymph, across the darkening brain.
I dream of reason and the first grows strong,
Drunk as a whirlwind on the sweating grain;
I dream of drunkenness and, freed from strain,
The second murmurs like a fingered gong;
I sink beneath the dream: his words grow sane,
Her pupils glow with pleasure all night long.

JOHN MONTAGUE
b. 1929

LATE

I return late, on tiptoe.
Moonlight pours over the bed
and your still, sleeping head
reproving silently
my stealthy prowler's tread.

CHILD

for Úna

A firefly gleams, then
fades upon your cheek.
Now you hide beneath
everything I write;
love's invisible ink,
heart's watermark.

JOHN MONTAGUE

from
THE CAVE OF NIGHT

FALLS FUNERAL

Unmarked faces
fierce with grief

a line of children
led by a small coffin

the young
mourning the young

a sight beyond tears
beyond pious belief

David's brethren
in the Land of Goliath.

TOM MACINTYRE
b. 1933

CATHLEEN

Lovely whore though,
Lovely, lovely whore,
And choosy –
Slept with Conn,
Slept with Niall,
Slept with Brian,
Slept with Rory.

Slide then,
The long slide.

Of course it shows.

AFTER THE IRISH
of Owen Roe O'Sullivan, eighteenth century

JAMES SIMMONS
b. 1933

A BIRTHDAY POEM

for Rachael

For every year of life we light
a candle on your cake
to mark the simple sort of progress
anyone can make,
and then, to test your nerve or give
a proper view of death,
you're asked to blow each light, each year,
out with your own breath.

JAMES SIMMONS

IN MEMORIAM: JUDY GARLAND

At forty-seven Frances Gumm is dead,
a plump, unhappy child who got ahead.

Towards the moon from her ecstatic face
notes soared. The moon is an awful place.

Discs are turning. Needles touch the rings
of dark rainbows. Judy Garland sings.

JAMES SIMMONS

FOR JAN BETLEY

The sad river passes
through melancholy glades
where leaves are silenced. It is late.

Under damp grasses
under the mist and trees, grenades
are stored in boxes, and will wait.

DESMOND EGAN
b. 1936

from
POEMS FOR NORTHERN IRELAND

THE NORTHERN IRELAND QUESTION

two *wee girls*
were playing tig near a car . . .

how many counties would you say
are worth their scattered fingers?

BRENDAN KENNELLY
b. 1936

THE GIFT

It came slowly.
Afraid of insufficient self-content,
Or some inherent weakness in itself,
Small and hesitant,
Like children at the tops of stairs,
It came through shops, rooms, temples,
Streets, places that were badly-lit,
It was a gift that took me unawares,
And I accepted it.

KATE ALLEN
b. 1937

VACUUM CLEANER

If it could blow them into shape
As well as suck them in,
The grit, the fluff, the scrap of tape,
The paper-flake, the pin
Would make an artificial flower
To justify the din.

SEAMUS HEANEY
b. 1939

WIDGEON

for Paul Muldoon

It had been badly shot.
While he was plucking it
he found, he says, the voice box –

like a flute stop
in the broken windpipe –

and blew upon it
unexpectedly
his own small widgeon cries.

SONG

A rowan like a lipsticked girl.
Between the by-road and the main road
Alder trees at a wet and dripping distance
Stand off among the rushes.

There are the mud-flowers of dialect
And the immortelles of perfect pitch
And that moment when the bird sings very close
To the music of what happens.

AN AUGUST NIGHT

His hands were warm and small and knowledgeable.
When I saw them again last night, they were two
    ferrets,
Playing all by themselves in a moonlit field.

SEAMUS HEANEY

THE STRAND

The dotted line my father's ashplant made
On Sandymount Strand
Is something else the tide won't wash away.

MICHAEL LONGLEY
b. 1939

KINDERTOTENLIEDER

There can be no songs for dead children
Near the crazy circle of explosions,
The splintering tangent of the ricochet,

No songs for the children who have become
My unrestricted tenants, fingerprints
Everywhere, teethmarks on this and that.

MICHAEL LONGLEY

THE GHOST ORCHID

Added to its few remaining sites will be the stanza
I compose about leaves like flakes of skin, a colour
Dithering between pink and yellow, and then the root
That grows like coral among shadows and leaf-litter.
Just touching the petals bruises them into darkness.

MICHAEL LONGLEY

OUT THERE

Do they ever meet out there,
The dolphins I counted,
The otter I wait for?
I should have spent my life
Listening to the waves.

MICHAEL LONGLEY

THE CENOTAPH

They couldn't wait to remember and improvised
A cenotaph of snow and a snowman soldier.
Inscribing *Lest We Forget* with handfuls of stones.

MICHAEL LONGLEY

A PRAYER

In our country they are desecrating churches.
May the rain that pours in pour into the font.
Because no snowflake ever falls in the wrong place,
May snow lie on the altar like an altar-cloth.

MICHAEL HARTNETT
1941–1999

THE LAST VISION OF
EOGHAN RUA Ó SÚILLEABHÁIN

The cow of morning spurted
milk-mist on each glen
and the noise of feet came
from the hills' white sides.
I saw like phantoms
my fellow-workers
and instead of spades and shovels
they had roses on their shoulders.

MICHAEL HARTNETT

from
INCHICORE HAIKU

What do bishops take
when the price of bread goes up?
A vow of silence.

DEREK MAHON
b. 1941

A DYING ART

'That day would skin a fairy –
A dying art,' she said.
Not many left of the old trade.
Redundant and remote, they age
Gracefully in dark corners
With lamp-lighters, sail-makers
And native Manx speakers.

And the bone-handled knives with which
They earned their bread? My granny grinds
Her plug tobacco with one to this day.

DEREK MAHON

NOSTALGIAS

The chair squeaks in a high wind,
Rain falls from its branches;
The kettle yearns for the mountain,
The soap for the sea.
In a tiny stone church
On a desolate headland
A lost tribe is singing 'Abide With Me'.

DEREK MAHON

from
LIGHT MUSIC

PLEASE

I built my house
in a forest far
from the venal roar.

Somebody please
beat a path
to my door.

DEREK MAHON

from
LIGHT MUSIC

DONEGAL

The vast clouds migrate
above turf-stacks
and a dangling gate.

A tiny bike squeaks
into the wind.

DEREK MAHON

from
LIGHT MUSIC

ROGUE LEAF

Believe it or not
I hung on all winter
outfacing wind and snow.

Now that spring
comes and the birds sing
I am letting go.

JOAN NEWMANN
b. 1942

THE LESSON

for Paula Meehan

I am reclining on my aunt Carrie.
Each time she speaks I push a finger
Into her mouth: finally she bites me.

GEOFFREY SQUIRES
b. 1942

'HOW IRRELEVANT CHILDHOOD SEEMS . . .'

How irrelevant childhood seems
and far away
I remember great trees
and darkness and being carried
upstairs. The wee *leiri*,
wind, snow blocking the lane
grandmother dead in the spare room

GEOFFREY SQUIRES

'EVERY LEAF IS WET . . .'

Every leaf is wet
and the fox hurries to his destination

small worlds of rain
on a grass-blade
shaken by a spider at work again

GEOFFREY SQUIRES

'IN CALIFORNIA
I HARDLY THOUGHT ABOUT HOME . . .'

In California I hardly thought about home
now suddenly I'm homesick
after three months
after a shower of rain
water everywhere, clarity
of blues and greens, bright clouds
in road-pools

GEOFFREY SQUIRES

'A GIRL . . .'

A girl
washing her hair
in the courtyard
with basins of cold water
under the stars

GEOFFREY SQUIRES

'HOW GOOD TO HAVE THE HOUSE QUIET . . .'

How good to have the house quiet
all to myself again, to be able to walk
towards a room and know
I shall be the only one there
no movement except my movement
no sounds except the sounds I make

PADRAIG J. DALY
b. 1943

Ó BRUADAIR: DEATH OF A YOUNG FRIEND

If only I had died before him;
His heart's pulse was my heart's life.

He was a hawk above the hillside,
An otter in the racing waters,

His breast pale as froth on a wave of the sea,
His limbs lissom and long and limber.

Until we meet again on the crowded mountain,
However long my life may be,
I will have lamentation on my lips.

THE PIETÀ
OF VILLENEUVE-LÉS-AVIGNON

With immense tenderness, they stretch his body out;
His limp hand falls to the ground.

One begins to anoint him with spices;
Another tenderly removes the thorns from his head.

How can we withhold our tears?
He is all our innocent pain.

PADRAIG J. DALY

YEAR'S ENDING

The crows gather to repossess the woods,
The river follows its silvery way,
The mountains begin to slip into darkness.

Soon only the sky will be real
And the houses pressed like tinsel stars
Onto the rim of the hill.

PAUL DURCAN
b. 1944

AUGHAWALL GRAVEYARD

Lonely lonely lonely lonely:
The story with a middle only.

PAUL DURCAN

IRELAND 1972

Next to the fresh grave of my beloved grandmother
The grave of my firstlove murdered by my brother.

ANTHONY GLAVIN
b. 1945

from
LIVING IN HIROSHIMA

LOVERS

They crawl through charred bamboo to the river's edge.
The water is hot to touch, but they slither in

And stroke and hold. At each caress, the skin
Dries instantly, then glows, then splits like porcelain.

TOM MATTHEWS
b. 1945

ADJUSTED

You are a well adjusted person
Every day you get adjusted to a new pain
You spend your evenings alone
With your body thinking of its long bones

TOM MATTHEWS

EVEN THE WHALES

Even the whales now
communicate sparingly with staccato cries
Polyphony was yesterday's song
We are minimalists
now, even the whales.

TOM MATTHEWS

THE POET WITH BAD TEETH

Pale as death
And deathly loitering

We smell his breath
And hear him muttering

He is the poet with bad teeth
We are not listening

BERNARD O'DONOGHUE
b. 1945

GOING WITHOUT SAYING

i.m. Joe Flynn

It is a great pity we don't know
When the dead are going to die
So that, over a last companionable
Drink, we could tell them
How much we liked them.

Happy the man who, dying, can
Place his hand on his heart and say:
'At least I didn't neglect to tell
The thrush how beautifully she sings.'

JOHN BOLAND
b. 1946

SAFE SEX

Afterwards, from one
or both of you,

will come a whispered
Are you OK?

as if you had just
been in an accident

and were checking
to see who'd survived.

MICHAEL FOLEY
b. 1947

THE POWER OF WORDS TO EXPRESS FEELINGS

When she left him he couldn't find a single word
   And when she came back one sufficed.
Christ, it was. *Christ! Oh Christ!*
   Blessed is he that comes in the name of the Lord.

DERMOT HEALY

b. 1947

TWO MOONS

The moon above Sligo
Is not
The moon above Mayo.

COLOURS

You'd be surprised
how black black is
when it's blue with rain.

And what do you do with the light
that comes in off the sea?
You might as well

forget what you look like
before you could ever begin
walking in it.

DERMOT HEALY

FIRE

in memory of Aidan

If you let the fire die
the soul scurries across the field
like a burning coal
off to another hearth.

Oh disloyal soul
separated from me
in my cold house!

THE PRAYER

for Noel Kilgallon

When Peggy was dying
her son leaned over to whisper
the Our Father into her ear.

She opened her eyes.
'Things must be bad,' she said,
'that you've started praying.'

TOM PAULIN

b. 1949

POT BURIAL

He has married again. His wife
Buys ornaments and places them
On the dark sideboard. Year by year
Her vases and small jugs crowd out
The smiles of the wife who died.

TOM PAULIN

OF DIFFERENCE DOES IT MAKE

*During the fifty-one-year existence of the
Northern Ireland parliament only one bill
sponsored by a non-Unionist member was ever passed.*

Among the plovers and the stonechats
protected by the Wild Birds Act
of nineteen-hundred-and-thirty-one,
there is a rare stint called the notawhit
that has a schisty flight-call, like the chough's.
Notawhit, notawhit, notawhit
– it raps out a sharp code sign
like a mild and patient prisoner
pecking through granite with a teaspoon.

MEDBH McGUCKIAN
b. 1950

SMOKE

They set the whins on fire along the road.
I wonder what controls it, can the wind hold
That snake of orange motion to the hills,
Away from the houses?

They seem so sure what they can do.
I am unable even
To contain myself, I run
Till the fawn smoke settles on the earth.

MEDBH McGUCKIAN

FELICIA'S CAFÉ

Darkness falls short by an hour
Of this summer's inhibitions:
Only the cold carpet
That owns a kind of flower,
Feeds any farm or ocean
Around the bedroom's heart.

Each day of brown perfection
May be colour enough for bees:
The part of my eye
That is not golden, sees.

PETER FALLON

b. 1951

THE HERD

I studied in the hedge school
and learned religions are a cod.
They're all the one.
Ask any fool.
Every lamb's a lamb of God.

PAUL MULDOON
b. 1951

BLEMISH

Were it indeed an accident of birth
That she looks on the gentle earth
And the seemingly gentle sky
Through one brown, and one blue eye.

PAUL MULDOON

IRELAND

The Volkswagen parked in the gap,
But gently ticking over.
You wonder if it's lovers
And not men hurrying back
Across two fields and a river.

PAUL MULDOON

from

HOPEWELL HAIKU

A stone at its core,
this snowball's the porcelain
knob on winter's door.

PAUL MULDOON

from
HOPEWELL HAIKU

The first day of spring.
What to make of that bald patch
right under the swing?

PAUL MULDOON

from
HOPEWELL HAIKU

Jean paints one toenail.
In a fork of the white ash,
quick, a cardinal.

GERALD DAWE
b. 1952

THE THIRD SECRET

The seas on either side of us
are slowly meeting, so they say.

I think we are quite simply
returning to constituent parts,

whether long in the tooth
or weak in the heart.

NUALA NÍ DHÓMHNAILL
b. 1952

from
CARNIVAL

I spent all last night
driving down the byroads of your parish
in an open sports car
without you near me.
I went past your house
and glimpsed your wife
in the kitchen.
I recognise the chapel
at which you worship.

translated from Irish by Paul Muldoon

NUALA NÍ DHÓMHNAILL

from
CARNIVAL

You won't hear a cheep from me.
That cat has got my tongue.
My hands do all the talking.
They're a swimming cap about your head
to protect you from the icy currents.
They're butterflies searching for sustenance
over your body's meadow.

translated from Irish by Paul Muldoon

WILLIAM PESKETT
b. 1952

CROM – APRIL 1969

the lake plane slices
the land from its reflection
like a fin

on a still day
there is twice as much of everything
except ripples

WILLIAM PESKETT

BIRTH AND DEATH

Birth and death,
my strict parentheses,
like two old friends in a crowd
you are struggling,
tending to meet

and like two adjacent tyrant kings
you are threatening
my life's expansion
and filling my head
with only me.

MAURICE SCULLY
b. 1952

A WALK-ON PART

Sexton Lund's daughter
Who was at school with Ibsen recalls
Three-quarters of a century later,
That he sometimes arrived in a red woolen cap.

When there was snow on the ground its top
She says, could be seen over the wall
Of the bridge he had to cross well
Before he himself
                    being small
Came into sight.

JULIE O'CALLAGHAN
b. 1954

PAPER SHORTAGE

Don't make excuses
about how difficult it is
to find a sheet
of delicate red-tinted Chinese paper.

Send a message
on a flat white pebble
or the stem of a hollyhock.
Etch your words
on a purple lotus petal.

DENNIS O'DRISCOLL
b. 1954

HOME

when all is said and done
what counts is having someone
you can phone at five to ask

for the immersion heater
to be switched to 'bath'
and the pizza taken from the deepfreeze

DENNIS O'DRISCOLL

from
CHURCHYARD VIEW:
THE NEW ESTATE

The child's coffin
like a violin case.
A pitch where parents' ears
can hear through clay.

TONY CURTIS
b. 1955

from
NORTHERN HAIKU

Shot twice in the head.
Once in each astonished eye.
History is blind.

TONY CURTIS

STILLNESS

On still nights I hear
the songs my grandmother sang:
three sad songs of home.

PAULA MEEHAN

b. 1955

'WOULD YOU JUMP INTO MY GRAVE AS QUICK?'

Would you jump into my grave as quick?
my granny would ask when one of us took
her chair by the fire. You, woman,
done up to the nines, red lips a come on,
your breath reeking of drink
and your black eye on my man tonight
in a Dublin bar, think
first of the steep drop, the six dark feet.

SEÁN DUNNE

1956–1995

from
LETTER TO LISBON

Once I flicked a crumb
From your skirt in a restaurant.
What lies I make my hands tell:
What could I care for crumbs?
It was you I wanted to touch.

SEÁN DUNNE

from
STILL LIVES

Your smell stays in the sheets.
I lie on your side of the bed
And inhale our last love-making,
The memory opening like a cave
Towards which I swell and surge
As your lost cries mingle with bells.

SEÁN DUNNE

from

TIME AND THE ISLAND

for Diarmuid Ó Drisceoil

THE PACT

When she left the island and married
Into Schull, she made her husband swear
To bury her on Cape when the time came.
When she died, boats carried
Her corpse beneath cliffs and sailed
In the shape of a cross on the open sea
With her bright coffin at its core,
And her husband near it to guide her home.

CHRIS AGEE
b. 1956

PORT OF BELFAST

Hung on a wall of Calvinist stars,
the moon is a mottled goatskin bodhran,
a vellum of weathered light
above the fog and frost of Lagan dips.

MOYRA DONALDSON
b. 1956

INFIDELITIES

After he'd gone,
she found money in the sheets,
fallen when he pulled his trousers off.
Gathering the coins into a small pile
she set them on the window ledge.
They sat, gathering dust, guilt,
until one day her husband
scooped them into his pocket.
Small change for a call
he couldn't make from the house.

AIDAN CARL MATHEWS
b. 1956

THE DEATH OF IRISH

The tide gone out for good,
Thirty-one words for seaweed
Whiten on the foreshore.

AIDAN CARL MATHEWS

from
BASHO'S REJECTED JOTTINGS

for Bill Brown

LIBRARIES

Culture, calm, and so forth.
I could go on.

Two desks down,
She's kicked off her shoes.

AIDAN CARL MATHEWS

from
BASHO'S REJECTED JOTTINGS

LIGHTS-OUT

I'm in luck –
Her nightdress still

Folded up
In the pink rabbit.

AIDAN CARL MATHEWS

from
BASHO'S REJECTED JOTTINGS

UNFINISHED HAIKU

Someone rang
At the crucial moment.
Never mind.

from
BASHO'S REJECTED JOTTINGS

RECONCILIATION

When you come back,
Your hands smell
Of walking gloveless.

CATHAL Ó SEARCAIGH
b. 1956

EXILE'S RETURN

for Peigí Rose

He's back tonight to a deserted house.
On the doorstep, under a brilliant moon, a stark
shadow: the tree he planted years ago is an old tree.

translated by Seamus Heaney

CATHAL Ó SEARCAIGH

SEASONS

A heavy summer shower in the hills –
In the teeming downpour,
I hear a thousand cows being milked.

In the winter whiteness of the hills
thatch-eaves are heavy with frost –
from their teats, silence drips.

translated by Cathal Ó Searcaigh

CATHAL Ó SEARCAIGH

WORDS OF A BROTHER

for Ciarán and Fiona

'We are all brothers,'
the monk said to my father.
but when I countered
his flattering cliché –
'like Cain and Abel'

I had to shiver.
The fratricidal dagger of his stare
was deep in my breast.

translated by Thomas McCarthy

CATHAL Ó SEARCAIGH

KNOWLEDGE

Skin pressed to skin, my heart,
Salt of our sweat
Churning the sheets to a sea.

Mouth pressed firmly to mouth,
The salmon of knowledge – your tongue –
Tonight will swim in me.

translated by Gabriel Rosenstock

MICHAEL O'LOUGHLIN
b. 1958

from
THE SHARDS

THE BIRDS

Somewhere north of Lille
I stared at the sea of white crosses,
Like sea birds resting on the earth.
So much suddenly real!

DERMOT BOLGER
b. 1959

PRAYER

I have come this long way without finding you
Or losing your reflection,

And tried a dozen obsessions without cleansing
Your taste from my tongue.

Oldest friend and adversary, fugitive brother,
We recognise each other

In carriages of express trains which pass:
Your hands beat on the glass.

PETER SIRR
b. 1960

from
HOME BALLADS

A LESSON

You say
there is a language in which the word for family

is also the word for departure.
Handing across books, tapes, the world's

thinnest dictionary,
learn it, you say.

ANDREW ELLIOTT
b. 1961

HERE TODAY . . .

Making love down through the centuries
Men have left their shadow on women.

Nowadays I want the shadow I leave
To be that of a bird on the bed of a stream.

PÓL Ó MUIRÍ
b. 1965

A VISIT

It's not the sound of geese
Or watering the cattle
Or living in Clanrolla North
That I find odd.

It's ringing my parents
To alert them to a visit:
The married son and wife
Making an appointment.

I no longer have a key
For my parents' home.

PÓL Ó MUIRÍ

PADRE PIO

At San Giovanni, we rested after the invasion.
Padre Pio read the Mass, his hands hidden in
Gloves as he raised the chalice to the heavens.
I left to find Leather Tits, the prostitute, and
Spent a wondrous night, my body as her chalice,
Blood and tears seeping from my every young pore.

DAVID WHEATLEY
b. 1970

from
A PARIS NOTEBOOK

NOTHING TO DECLARE

My ears popped as the 737 cleared the tarmac,
unpopped again to the captain's *Céad Míle Fáilte* two miles up.

'Nothing to Declare' then: exchanging one Departure Lounge
for another as simply as I set my watch back an hour . . .

And reaching into my pocket in Dublin for busfare home
I found handfuls of marvellous, suddenly worthless coins.

SINEAD MORRISSEY
b. 1972

CLOTHES

Once they come undone, there's no stopping the undoing
Of all that keeps us us and not we.
From a room full of history and underwear
I throw out my diary and walk naked.

Until we're talking of weather again,
Contact shrunk back to wherever it sprang from.
And I'm begging for it all, coat, hat, gloves, scarf –
Shoes shod in iron, and a waterproof.

ACKNOWLEDGEMENTS

The editor and publisher gratefully acknowledge permission to include the following copyright material:

AGEE, CHRIS, 'Port of Belfast' from *In the New Hampshire Woods* (Dedalus Press, 1992), by permission of the author

ALLEN, FERGUS, 'Way Back Then' from *Who Goes There?* (Faber and Faber, 1996), by permission of Faber and Faber

ALLEN, KATE, 'Vacuum Cleaner', by permission of the author

BECKETT, SAMUEL, 'I would like my love to die' from *Collected Poems in English and French* (John Calder (Publishers) Ltd, 1972), by permission of The Calder Educational Trust and the Estate of Samuel Beckett and Grove/Atlantic Inc. Copyright © Samuel Beckett, 1972

BEHAN, BRENDAN, 'Loneliness' from *Poems and a Play in Irish* (Gallery Press, 1981), by permission of the Tessa Sayle Agency

BOLAND, JOHN, 'Safe sex' from *Brow Head* (Abbey Press, 1999), by permission of Abbey Press

BOLGER, DERMOT, 'Prayer' from *Taking My Letters Back: New and Selected Poems* (New Island, 1998), by permission of New Island Books

CLARKE, AUSTIN, 'Penal Law' from *Collected Poems* (Dolmen Press, 1974), permission granted by R. Dardis Clarke, 21 Pleasants Street, Dublin 8

CURTIS, TONY, an extract from 'Northern Haiku' from *This far North* (Dedalus Press, 1994), by permission of Dedalus Press.

DALY, PADRAIG J., 'Ó Bruadair: Death of a Young Friend' from *Out of Silence* (Dedalus Press, 1993), by permission of Dedalus Press

ACKNOWLEDGEMENTS

HARVEY, FRANCIS, 'Storm Petrel' from *The Boa Island Janus* (Dedalus Press, 1996), by permission of Dedalus Press

HEALY, DERMOT, 'Two Moons' from *The Ballyconnell Colours* (Gallery Press, 1992), by kind permission of the author and The Gallery Press

HEANEY, SEAMUS, 'Song', 'Widgeon', 'An August Night' and 'The Strand' from *Opened Ground: Poems 1966–1996* (Faber and Faber, 1998 and Farrar, Straus and Giroux, 1998). Copyright © 1998 by Seamus Heaney, reprinted by permission of Faber and Faber and Farrar, Straus and Giroux, LLC

HEWITT, JOHN, 'Lyric', 'Chinese Fluteplayer' and 'Grey and White' from *The Collected Poems of John Hewitt* (Blackstaff Press, 1991), by permission of the Blackstaff Press on behalf of the Estate of John Hewitt

KAVANAGH, PATRICK, 'Sanctity' and 'Consider the Grass Growing' from *Selected Poems* (Penguin, 1996), reprinted with the permission of the Trustees of the Estate of the late Katherine B. Kavanagh, through the Jonathan Williams Literary Agency

KENNELLY, BRENDAN, 'The Gift' from *A Time for Voices: Selected Poems 1960–1990* (Bloodaxe, 1990), by permission of Bloodaxe

KINSELLA, THOMAS, 'Fire and Ice' from *Collected Poems* (Oxford University Press, 1996), by permission of the author and Carcanet Press Limited

LONGLEY, MICHAEL, 'Kindertotenlieder' from *Selected Poems* (Jonathan Cape, 1991) and *Michael Longley: Poems 1963–1983* (Wake Forest University Press, 1985); 'The Ghost Orchid' and 'Out There' from *Selected Poems* (Jonathan Cape, 1991 and Wake Forest University Press, 1999); and 'The Cenotaph' and 'A Prayer' from *The Weather in Japan* (Jonathan Cape, 2000 and Wake Forest University Press, 2000), by permission of Random House UK Ltd and Wake Forest University Press

McGUCKIAN, MEDBH, 'Felicia's Café' from *Venus and the Rain* (Gallery Press, 1984/1994), and 'Smoke' from *The Flower Master and Other Poems* (Gallery Press, 1993), by kind permission of the author and The Gallery Press

MacINTYRE, TOM, 'Cathleen' from *I Bailed Out at Ardee* (Dedalus Press, 1987), by permission of the author

MacNEICE, LOUIS, 'Coda', 'Corner Seat' and 'Nightclub' from *Collected Poems* (Faber and Faber, 1966), by permission of the Estate of Louis MacNeice and Faber and Faber

MAHON, DEREK, 'A Dying Art', 'Nostalgias' and extracts from 'Light Music' from *Collected Poems* (Gallery Press, 1999), by kind permission of the author and The Gallery Press

MATHEWS, AIDAN CARL, 'The Death of Irish' and extracts from 'Basho's Rejected Jottings' from *Minding Ruth* (Gallery Press, 1983), by kind permission of the author and The Gallery Press

MATTHEWS, TOM, 'Adjusted', 'The Poet with Bad Teeth' and 'Even the Whales' from *Dr Wilson as an Arab* (Holysmoke Press, 1974), by permission of the author

MEEHAN, PAULA, 'Would you jump into my grave as quick?' from *Pillow Talk* (Gallery Press, 1994), by kind permission of the author and The Gallery Press

MONTAGUE, JOHN, extracts from 'The Cave of Night' from *John Montague: Collected Poems* (Gallery Press, 1995 and Wake Forest University Press, 1995), by kind permission of the author and The Gallery Press and Wake Forest University Press

MORRISSEY, SINEAD, 'Clothes' from *There was a Fire in Vancouver* (Carcanet Press, 1996), by kind permission of Carcanet Press Limited

MULDOON, PAUL, 'Blemish' from *Mules* (Faber and Faber, 1977 and Wake Forest University Press, 1977) and 'Ireland' from *Why Brownlee Left* (Faber and Faber, 1980 and Wake Forest University Press, 1980), reprinted by permission of Faber and

ACKNOWLEDGEMENTS

Faber and Wake Forest University Press. Extracts from
'Hopewell Haiku' from *Hay* (Faber and Faber, 1998, and
Farrar, Straus and Giroux, 1998). Copyright © 1998 by Paul
Muldoon, reprinted by permission of Faber and Faber and
Farrar, Straus and Giroux, LLC

MURPHY, RICHARD, 'Lullaby' from *Collected Poems* (Gallery
Press, 2000) and *Richard Murphy: Collected Poems* (Wake
Forest University Press, 2000), by kind permission of the
author and The Gallery Press and Wake Forest University
Press

NEWMANN, JOAN, 'The Lesson' from *Thin Ice* (Abbey Press,
1998), by permission of Abbey Press

NÍ DHÓMHNAILL, NUALA, extracts from 'Carnival' (translated
by Paul Muldoon) from *The Astrakhan Cloak* (Gallery Press,
1992 and Wake Forest University Press, 1993), by kind
permission of the author and The Gallery Press and Wake
Forest University Press

O'CALLAGHAN, JULIE, 'Paper Shortage' from *No Can Do*
(Bloodaxe, 2000), by permission of Bloodaxe Books

O'CONNOR, FRANK, 'Advice to Lovers' from *The Little
Monasteries* (Dolmen Press, 1963), and 'The King of
Connacht' from *Kings, Lords and Commons* (Gill and
Macmillan, 1961), reprinted by permission of PFD on behalf
of The Estate of Frank O'Connor. Copyright © Frank
O'Connor 1961, 1963

O'DONOGHUE, BERNARD, 'Going Without Saying' from
Gunpowder (Chatto and Windus, 1995), by permission of
Random House UK Ltd

O'DRISCOLL, DENNIS, an extract from 'Breviary' from *Quality
Time* (Anvil Press Poetry, 1997), and an extract from
'Churchyard View: The New Estate' from *Weather Permitting*
(Anvil Press Poetry, 1999), by permission of Anvil Press
Poetry

O'LOUGHLIN, MICHAEL, an extract from 'The Shards' from

Another Nation: New and Selected Poems (New Island, 1996), by permission of New Island Books

Ó MUIRÍ, PÓL, 'A Visit' and 'Padre Pio' from *D-Day* (Lagan Press, 1995), by permission of Lagan Press

Ó SEARCAIGH, CATHAL, 'Exiles Return', 'Seasons', 'Words of a brother' and 'Knowledge' from *Homecoming/An Bealach 'na Bhaile* (Cló Iar-Chonnachta, 1993), by permission of Cló Iar-Chonnachta

PAULIN, TOM, an extract from 'The Pot Burial' from *The Strange Museum* (Faber and Faber, 1980), and 'Of Difference Does it Make' from *Liberty Tree* (Faber and Faber, 1983), by permission of Faber and Faber

PESKETT, WILLIAM, 'Birth and Death' and 'Crom – April 1969' from *The Nightowl's Dissection* (Secker and Warburg, 1975), by permission of Random House UK Ltd

RODGERS, W.R., 'The Lovers' and 'The Fountains' from *Poems* (Gallery Press, 1993), by kind permission of the author and The Gallery Press

SCULLY, MAURICE, 'A Walk-On Part' from *Love Poems and Others* (Raven Arts, 1981), by permission of the author

SIMMONS, JAMES, 'A Birthday Poem', 'In Memoriam: Judy Garland' and 'For Jan Beatley' from *Poems 1956–1986* (Gallery Press, 1986), by kind permission of the author and The Gallery Press

SIRR, PETER, an extract from 'Home Ballads' from *The Ledger of Fruitful Exchange* (Gallery Press, 1995), by kind permission of the author and The Gallery Press

SQUIRES, GEOFFREY, 'How irrelevant childhood . . .', 'In California I hardly thought about home . . .', 'Every leaf is wet . . .', 'A girl . . .' and 'How good to have the house quiet . . .' from *Drowned Stones* (New Writers' Press, 1975), by permission of the author

WHEATLEY, DAVID, an extract from 'A Paris Notebook' from *Thirst* (Gallery Press, 1997), by kind permission of the

ACKNOWLEDGEMENTS

author and The Gallery Press

YEATS, W.B., 'A Drinking Song', 'After Long Silence', 'Memory',
'The Great Day' and 'The Spur' from *The Collected Poems of
W.B. Yeats* (Macmillan, 1937), by permission of A.P. Watt
Limited on behalf of Michael B. Yeats. 'A Drinking Song' and
'Memory' reprinted with the permission of Scribner, a
Division of Simon & Schuster from *The Collected Poems of
W.B. Yeats*, revised second edition edited by Richard
J. Finneran. Copyright 1940 by Georgie Yeats; copyright
renewed © 1968 by Bertha Georgie Yeats, Michael Butler
Yeats and Anne Yeats

INDEX OF TITLES

INDEX OF TITLES

INDEX OF FIRST LINES

THE HIP FLASK

144

INDEX OF FIRST LINES